A Ring-o'-Roses

Wendy Slater

Northcote House

By the same author

Teaching Modern Educational Dance

British Library Cataloguing Publication Data

Slater, Wendy
A ring-o'-roses : poems for dance and movement.
I. Title
821'.914   PZ8.3

ISBN 0-7463-0525-7

First published in 1989 by Northcote House Publishers Ltd, Harper & Row
House, Estover Road, Plymouth PL6 7PZ, United Kingdom. Tel: Plymouth
(0752) 705251. Telex: 45635. Fax: (0752) 777603.

Printed in Great Britain by BPCC Wheatons Ltd, Exeter

Preface

This book is intended for all those who like to use poetry, both as a stimulus and as a descriptive aid to the dance lesson. The poems have been written specifically for movement but this will, I hope, not preclude their use on other occasions.

I did not originally set out to write the poems especially for a book, but for use in my own dance lessons. Having found that I was continually being asked by teachers the source of my material, I realised that there was a need for poetry written specially for the movement situation. This prompted me to collect together the poems already written and to write, in addition, a selection of verse that I hope will prompt creative thought on a number of themes.

The poems are written primarily for use with junior and infant classes, but I hope that some might be found to be of use with older children and students.

✳ TEACHING

A Ring-o'-Roses

Literature

For Miss Grace Tilley and K. C.
—with grateful thanks

Contents

Fairytale world

Toyland

Bits and pieces

Introduction:
Using Poetry in the Dance Lesson

Words are a very valuable stimulus to the dance lesson and in every way as important as music or percussive sound. When we introduce poetry we extend the use of language a little further and offer the child a new medium for gaining creative experience.

If left to ourselves we would probably find that we all interpret poetry in different ways, just as we all hear the sounds differently when we listen to music. Poetry, like music, speaks, but it speaks to each one of us individually. The poems in this book will stimulate each one of us to plan our lessons in a different way. Many teachers have only used poetry infrequently, if at all, and I feel that it might be helpful to explore different types of poetry and their possible movement interpretation in greater depth.

For ease I am going to suggest four sections into which most poems, if not all, will fit — some in fact fitting comfortably into more than one category. They are as follows:

(a) descriptive poems
(b) dramatic poems
(c) poems suggesting pure movement ideas
(d) story poems.

Some of the poems may be used as an actual accompaniment to the climax of the lesson. Others will be read to awaken the child's awareness at some stage in the lesson but the climax itself may be a response to music or percussion.

(a) DESCRIPTIVE POEMS

These are probably the easiest to use in the dance lesson as they are generally read in order to set the scene or 'spark off' the children's interest in a particular subject. For instance, the poem entitled *Summer Magic* is intended to make the listener aware of the atmosphere and pleasure of a glorious summer day. It is a 'mood setter' and does not in itself suggest any particular movement idea. It could be used to encourage children to feel happy and carefree and to bring this out in their movement. Alternatively it might be used as part of a cycle of dances based on the

Descriptive	Dramatic	Pure movement	Story
Magic of Spring	Journey into Space	The Sun	Winter Fun
Summer Magic	A Witchy Tale	The Elephant and	Late for Work
Autumn Days	Strange Creatures	the Ant	Seaside Day
Leaves	Bonfire Night	Snake Song	Fairground
Wayward Wind	Tiny Wee	At Snail's Pace	
Winter Fun	Tight-tope Walker	Dancing Shoes	
A Sudden Storm		The Swing	
Raindrops		Bouncing Balls	
Beginnings		Mirror Game	
Kestrel		Machines	
My Flying Kite		Tiny Wee	
Catrina		Jerky the Puppet	
Balloon		My Magic Box	
Seaside Day		The Rocking Horse	
A Harvest Prayer		Walking	
		Giantland	
		Kangaroo Hop	

seasons in conjunction with stimuli from other art forms. In contrast, the poem *Autumn Days* is a descriptive poem which does suggest a variety of movements and shapes and could in fact be used as an accompaniment to the children's movement in the 'climax' section of the lesson. I have found that children respond extremely well to the actual words of a poem and to a teacher who can bring out the rhythms and changes of mood in her voice.

Many of these poems can be used as a stimulus for a single movement lesson but others may be the starting point for a scheme of work that involves not only a series of movement lessons but creates an opportunity for a follow through into the classroom subjects. This may take the form of discussion, creative writing, drama or art work. Conversely, a topic begun in the classroom can be enlarged upon and enriched if taken through into the dance lesson. For instance, the class teacher might be involved in a topic based on weather. This could be the starting point for movement lessons which explore the different qualities of movement involved in the various aspects of weather change, ie the light dabbing movements of a rain shower, the sharp spiky movements of a flash of lightning, the swirling whirling movements precipitant of hurricanes and gales, the gentle drifting movements of a breeze, and so on. Children may then be encouraged to write their own poems based on these themes.

The following suggested lessons are based on a day at the seaside and are stimulated by the poem *A Seaside Day*. Suggested music for this is the Theme from Music Boxtape No. 2, *The Sea*.

Lesson One

Main theme: Body awareness with emphasis on changing body shape.
Sub-themes: (a) Awareness of space—changes of direction, levels.
(b) Awareness of weight and time—contrasting spiky and smooth movement.
Relationship: Individual.

Introductory Activity
Jumping all over the room making an angular zig-zag pattern.

Movement Training
1. Walking with change of direction.
2. Running—tiny steps. Change of direction, high and low.
3. Using the hands to make a twisting curving pattern around the body.
4. Light running steps and twisting, curving hands together.
5. Make a spiky shape. Change suddenly from one spiky shape to another.
6. Travelling and stopping in different spiky shapes.
7. Curl up small. Grow slowly and smoothly into a stretched shape on your feet.

Climax
Read the poem to the children. Play the music for the dawn at sea and to finish the lesson let the children work at the slow, smooth growing to the music.

Lesson Two

Themes: As Lesson One.
Relationship: Individual moving into small groups of three.

Introductory Activity
Running with twisting curving hands that lead you high and low.

Movement Training
1. Walking stretched high up on toes.
2. Walking low down near to the floor.
3. Use your hands to take you on a pathway up and down like the rising and falling actions of the waves.
4. Revise growing smoothly and slowly into a stretched shape (to music).

Climax
In small groups of three. Two children to join together to make a jagged, spiky rock shape whilst the other moves around them with the twisting, curving movements of the fish. (Music—the first section of music for waves.)

Lesson Three

Themes: As Lesson One.
Relationship: As Lesson Two.

Introductory Activity
Jumping all over the room making a pattern with feet sometimes close together and sometimes far apart.

Movement Training
1.   Hopping—changing feet to a regular rhythm.
2.   Small running steps, hands leading high and low.
3.   Travelling and stopping in stretched shapes.
4.   Running and jumping, making stretched shapes in the air.
5.   Travelling making a curving, twisting pattern all over the room. Stop and make a spiky shape with those close to you.

Climax
Join together the sunrise and the movements of fish around the rock shapes practiced in the previous two lessons. With the children, have a discussion about the movements and action of the waves and choose four large groups ready to begin work in the next lesson.

Lesson Four

Themes: As Lesson One.
Relationship: Four large groups.

Introductory Activity
Skipping with spiky feet that shoot out all around you.

Movement Training
1.   Walking with slow, careful steps.
2.   Walking with sharp, spiky heels, toes and sides of feet that shoot out around you.

3.   Running and jumping making stretched shapes in the air (like huge waves crashing against rocks).
4.   Keeping low to the floor, move in an undulating gentle way like the ripple of waves to the shore on a calm day.
5.   Travel with hands that lead you up and down and then drag you backwards (suggesting middle-sized waves as they travel to the shore and then are pulled back from the sand to join the sea again).

Climax
In four groups let the children put together their own ideas for the movements of the waves. Give help with suggestions of the various formations in which they can begin, ie lines, circles, smaller groups within the larger one each representing a different type of wave. Accompany the children's group work with the music called *Waves*. This is very general and can be used just as a background to the movements.

Lesson Five

Themes: As Lesson One.
Relationship: Individual.

Introductory Activity
Hopping all over the room making zig-zag patterns with your other knee.

Movement Training
1.   Running, making a twisting, curving pathway.
2.   Travelling and stopping in spiky shapes.
3.   Running and jumping, making sharp jagged shapes in the air.
4.   Keeping low to the floor, how many different ways of rolling can you find?
5.   Join together in sequences the spiky jumps and different ways of rolling to represent flashes of lightning and rolls of thunder.
6.   Fill the room with movement travelling high and low — swirling, whirling, jumping, rolling, spinning (the storm at its peak).

Climax
Let the children listen to the music for the storm. The children may either be left free to interpret the idea as they wish, drawing on ideas presented in the lesson, or the teacher may wish to organise this into pairs or some sort of group work.

Lesson Six

Themes: As Lesson One.
Relationship: Individual.

Introductory Activity
Running and jumping, making stretched, spiky or curled shapes in the air.

Movement Training
1.   Revision of any aspects of movement from previous lessons.
2.   Imagine that you have a heavy object in front of you. Can you push it away from you with a strong, slow movement?
3.   Imagine the same object with a rope tied round it. Can you find different ways of pulling that object along (hauling in the boats)?
4.   Work again at smooth, slow growing into stretched shapes and gentle sustained movements that sink back into a small shape.

Climax
At the end of the storm music there is a section suitable for pulling in the boats. This is followed by the slow section for *Calm* after the storm. The children may use this for curling up slowly to represent the sunset.

These six lessons can be used to explore a different section of the poem each week. They are, however, the bare bones of a much larger scheme whereby the poem is built onto in each lesson and at the end the children dance it in its entirety.

(b) DRAMATIC POEMS

Poems that come under this heading are much more concerned with the creation of an atmosphere rather than describing an event or a sensation. They are designed to propel the imagination of a child into an event which either has its roots in reality (ie *A Witchy Tale*) or into a situation where most children can only spectate and draw from the atmosphere rather than be an active participant (ie *The Tight-rope Walker*).

These poems are designed to open the child's mind to realms that are outside his experience rather than open his eyes to our everyday world. In the descriptive section we aim to bring the child to a greater awareness of his surroundings. Dramatic poems bring the child into a world where the exciting and unusual happen. They take him to visit unheard of planets to meet strange creatures, to visit the realms of giants and elves. They are poems of fantasy and fairytale as necessary to the young child as the world he knows and lives in.

The following example is a lesson based on the use of the poem *A Witchy Tale*, suitable for top infants and first-year juniors.

Lesson One

Main theme: Awareness of weight and time, emphasising the contrast between spiky and smooth movements.
Sub-themes: (a) Body awareness — sharp, spiky movements of different body parts.
(b) Space awareness — changing levels, on the spot and travelling.
Relationship: Dancing alone.

Introductory Activity
Skipping all over the room with knees that shoot out around you.

Movement Training
1.   Walking all over the room, remembering change of direction and floor pattern.
2.   Walking with slow, careful, creeping steps.
3.   Walking on different parts of the feet, ie toes, heels, insides and outsides.
4.   Walking with spiky steps, shooting the feet out into the spaces.

Sitting
5.   Heads that move in a smooth and curving way.
6.   Sharp, jerky movements of heads in different directions.
7.   Hands that shake into the spaces all around you.
8.   Choose one hand to be the leader. This hand makes smooth, gentle, curving patterns around the body while the other follows it. Emphasise children watching hands wherever they go.
9.   Sharp, spiky movements of fingers, wrists, elbows and heads into the spaces around the body.

Standing
10.   Can you do a spiky dance with every part of you — shooting fingers and feet out into all the spaces as you travel all over the room.
11.   Small shape. Growing slowly and smoothly into a stretched shape balanced on any part of your body.
12.   Grow in a spiky way, shooting up bit by bit until you are in a spiky shape on your feet. Curl up again as quickly as you can.

Climax
Read the children the poem *A Witchy Tale*. The movement is best done

using the words of the poem itself as an accompaniment. The children grow in a spiky way to the words 'The witches begin to wake' . They do their spiky dance all over the room, curling up quickly on the words 'Everyone will disappear' . The children should be encouraged to make their movements witch-like and to use facial expression as well.

I have suggested only one lesson where all the children interpret the movement of the witches. This could, however, be enlarged into a longer theme where the class divides — some to take the part of the witches and others to work on the movements and the story of those who are creeping through the woods at midnight, to spy on the witches' party.

(c) PURE MOVEMENT

These are poems which were written not to enhance the senses or the imagination of the child but as an aid to the exploration of the more functional aspects of movements. We base our theories of movement on certain clearly defined concepts:

- Which parts of us can move?
- Where can they go in the space around us?
- How do they move?
- What is the relationship in movement of one body part to another and what relationship has the whole body to other people with whom it shares a space?

These poems are designed to help the child to be more aware of the possibilities of movement within his own body. They begin at their most simple with poems like *Walking*. This is intended to stimulate young infants to explore the many different ways in which the feet can indulge in a simple activity like stepping. The poem itself can be used as an accompaniment to the climax of the lesson with the children matching their steps to the words of each verse. It is concerned primarily with which part of the body is moving. This idea is extended a little further in the poem *Dancing Shoes*, again intended for young infants.

We now explore other ways of using the feet in addition to walking. We begin to examine *where* the feet are going to move to; an introduction to the awareness of space around us. The poem mentions the directions of forwards, backwards, sideways, around, and explores the differences between movements that travel and movements that stay on the spot. The poems *Giantland* and *Tiny Wee* suggest the difference between small and large movements, whereas the poem *The Elephant and the Ant* is concerned with the awareness of speed and the difference between sustained, gradual movements and those which are quick and sudden. These are the beginning of an exploration into the quality of movement. This lesson, based on the poem *The Sun*, embodies all four aspects of pure movement stimuli.

Lesson One

Main theme: Body awareness, with emphasis on movements of heads, hands and feet; wide and tall shapes.
Sub-themes: (a) Space awareness — change of level with rising, sinking and travelling.
(b) Awareness of weight and time, slow and light movement contrasted with quick and light movement.

Introductory Activity
Running with tiny steps, remembering all the directions and high and low.

Movement Training
1.   Skipping with change of direction.
2.   Skipping with feet shooting out all around you.
3.   Travelling and stopping.
4.   Travelling and stopping in wide or tall shapes.

Sitting
5.   Hands shaking all around you.
6.   Gentle wriggling fingers into all the spaces.
7.   Hands that open and close very quickly.
8.   Skipping fingers around you, travelling high and low, in front, behind and out to the sides.
9.   Fingers that skip around you and feet that skip into the spaces at the same time.
10.   Make a small shape. Can you shoot like a rocket into a tall shape, or a wide shape, and curl up quickly again?
11.   Can you grow very slowly into your wide or tall shape and curl up again just as smoothly?

Climax
Read the poem to the children. The children can then dance to the words of the poem, growing slowly as the sun rises; dancing with skippy fingers and feet as the sun travels across the sky; curling up smoothly and gently as the sun sets.

(d) STORY POEMS

These poems, though smaller in number, are intended to describe a series of events that may be within the child's experience but form a narrative. All will need to be used as the theme for a series of lessons. It is possible that each lesson might explore a small section of the poem and yet be complete within itself. Alternatively, the story might be built up lesson by lesson to be performed as a whole at the end of the scheme with each part linking together in some way.

I have chosen the poem *Late for Work* as an example of the latter. Each part is performed to music as suggested below:

Waking — Scenes d'enfant. Listen, Move and Dance No 2 (HMV).
Getting Ready — No 6 for children. Listen, Move and Dance No 1 (HMV).
Signals — No 29 for children. Listen, Move and Dance No 1 (HMV).
Train — No 4, Electronic Sound Pictures. Listen, Move and Dance No 4 (HMV).
Horses — Gallop. Listen and Move No 5.
Going to the Buffet — Syncopated Tune. Listen and Move No 5.

The poem suggests a number of different movement ideas and the teacher might wish to select just a few of these to interpret in movement. I have not included a series of lesson plans for this dance, but below is a list of movement training suitable for each section:

Waking
The movement should be sustained and will include work on rising and sinking in different ways, gesture and body shapes. The children will begin in attitudes of sleep, low to the floor.

Getting ready
This movement is more mimetic, eg washing, cleaning teeth, getting dressed, running downstairs, putting on hat and coat, running to the station and stopping to cross the roads. This is a direct contrast with the sustained movement of *Waking*.

Signals
Sharp, angular movements into space with different parts of the body, ie elbow joint, shoulders, heads, knees, wrists. Whole body movements up and down, forwards and back or side to side suggesting the rise and fall of the signals.

Train
This music could be used as a sound effect to link two parts of the dance. Alternatively, part of the class may dance the movements of the train whilst others use it as a background to the hurry and bustle of people rushing to catch the train. The teacher could spend more time working on acceleration and deceleration in movement to suggest the arrival and departure of the train.

Horses
A simple galloping activity accenting the knees and the pathway on the floor.

Walking to the Buffet
Walking at different speeds and overbalancing movements with changes of direction and level. The children could mime having to climb over luggage, squeeze between pieces, lift it out of the way, etc.

IN CONCLUSION

The examples I have chosen are merely suggestions to give the teacher an idea of how poetry can be used as a stimulus and even as an accompaniment in the dance lesson or as the starting point for a theme both in the dance lesson or in the classroom situation. My examples are only intended as a starting point to whet the appetite and it is hoped that the poems will fire the imagination of both the teachers and the pupils to create their own movement experiences and to write their own poetry for dance.

1

The Magic of Spring

With a last flurry of snow
The long, dark days of winter are drawing to a close.
As if by some sweet magic, a smell of Spring is in the air,
Lightening our hearts and lifting care-worn spirits.
The once dead earth is live again,
With small, green shoots thrusting towards the light,
Then growing steadily upwards, opening bright faces
To reflect the sun.
Spring is the time for growing things,
Of sudden showers, when the sound of rain
Dripping from newly-opened leaves
Plays with the mad March wind
And makes the sky a patchwork quilt of cloud and blue.
The fields are bright with many-coloured flowers
Making a carpet for the playful new-born lambs
And the hurry and scurry of a mother hen around small, downy
 chicks.
The sound of busy, whirring wings is heard
As birds swoop overhead collecting 'this and that' to build their
 nests,
Preparing once again to rear their young.
Spring days are hopeful days, when young and old alike
Look forward to the warmer days of summer.

2

Summer Magic

Summer time,
With the high sun at noon
And the drone of a bee overhead.
Skies of blue
Dotted with white, fluffy clouds,
And birds rising and falling on the wing.

Warmth and peace
Of the quiet countryside
And nurturing the harvest crops.
Bright meadow flowers
Of white and shining gold
And here and there a touch of flaming red.

Placid rivers
Gently flowing their winding course
Past woods and thickets bursting leaf.
Lazy sheep,
And the gentle lowing of contented cows
Feeding from pastures rich with green.

Picnicking days,
For those in holiday mood
To gaze upon this beauty everywhere.
Nature's playground;
Where the wonders of her miracles
Play background to the glorious summer days.

3

Autumn Days

A gentle breeze ripples the leaves upon the trees,
Making them dance and flutter.
Gay colours, orange and red and brown,
Rustling and whispering, speaking of autumn days.
One by one they come floating down
To make rich-coloured carpets on the ground,
Crunching and crackling as we walk.
But when the wind blows hard and strong
It lifts the leaves and sends them whirling and twirling
First high, then low,
Scurrying and hurrying, nearer to winter days.
The trees, now bare, stand in their glory,
Shapes carved against November skies,
Still in their beauty, yet just waiting
For the first signs of spring
When the leaves will clothe them for another year.

4

Winter Fun

The snow kept falling through the night:
Crystal flakes of shimmering white
Came gently drifting, floating down
Upon the silent, sleeping town.

The children, playing out next day,
Keeping warm and feeling gay,
Make footprint patterns in the snow,
And we can see just where they go

As off into the woods they run,
Just watch and see how they have fun,
While snowballs hurtle through the air
And we all wish that we were there.

But someone else is watching, too:
It's old Jack Frost! What will he do?
He'll make them shiver, wait and see;
Poor frozen statues they will be!

Now in a quick dance off he goes,
Nipping at their hands and toes;
He's happy now he's found a way
To tease the children as they play.

But look! The sun comes out at last.
Our Jack Frost's merry game is past.
The warmth will melt him right away.
He'll have to play another day.

O how the time has quickly gone!
The children's games are nearly done.
The sun has almost left the sky
As happy voices call 'Goodbye!'

5

Seasons

In spring we plant our little seeds
And wait for them to grow.
They nestle snugly in the ground,
Safe from cold winds that blow.

Then comes the rain that makes them swell
And send out tiny roots;
While pushing strongly through the earth
We see the first green shoots.

They grow and grow through summer months
Warmed by the shining sun,
Until they reach their flowering time
And harvest time has come.

The farmers gather in the crops
And autumn comes again.
The leaves come tumbling from the trees
Leaving them bare and plain.

Now the winter time is here
And we must wait for spring again,
When new seeds will begin to grow
Fed by the sun and the gentle rain.

6

Leaves

In winter the trees stand bare and tall.
For months there aren't any leaves at all.
Then comes the spring with warmer days
When the sun begins to cast its rays
And young things start to grow.

On the branches of trees the buds appear
As they always do at this time of year.
Forgetting the winter, the wet and the cold,
The tiny leaves begin to unfold
And open and spread in the sun.

In summer the leaves are happy and gay,
With nothing to do but rustle and play.
But all too soon autumn days are here
Warning that winter again is near
And it's time for the leaves to fall.

One by one they come fluttering down
Making bright coloured carpets all over the town.
Then comes Mr. Wind with a whoop and a shout.
He lifts them and whirls them and twirls them about,
And flings them from place to place.

When the wind has finished and passes on
We find that most of the leaves have gone.
They have lost their colour and shrivelled up small,
And soon there'll be nothing to see at all
For the winter has come again.

7

The Wayward Wind

At first a cool, fresh breeze,
Rustling the leaves, and soft upon your face,
Playfully lifting small and downy things
And carrying them as if on wings
To put them down in a new hiding place.

Then comes a gust of wind,
Still playful, but on mischief bound,
Turning umbrellas inside out and outside in,
A game which only he can win
Until he passes on to break new ground.

But should that gust turn next into a gale,
Oh, what a very different tale he has to tell!
With temper rising, now he flings
So many things, both big and small, into the air;
Sending them spinning, whirling, twirling
Until he stops awhile to catch his breath
And they come to rest on solid earth once more.

Sometimes the wind forgets to take his time,
And rising, swelling, ever stronger yet, a rampant lion he becomes,
Uprooting trees and tossing cars
As if they were but cardboard toys.
The hurricane is not a playful friend:
He is the harbinger of death;
A force that man, so frail, cannot yet tame.

Where now that gentle breeze, so cool,
Rustling the leaves and soft upon your face?
The elements and man have battled many times,
Yet we cannot contain the rebel wind
When he blows from out of space.

8

A Sudden Storm

At dawn a gentle breeze began to blow,
Which as the day progressed grew stronger, 'til
It now became a raging gale;
And with the wind came rain.
A large drop fell, hard on the dusty ground,
Then more and more, until the rain came bouncing down,
Hitting the pavements with a short, sharp slap,
Faster and faster 'til it seemed to drum upon the ears,
Until as suddenly as it started
Then it stopped.
As daylight faded the temperature began to fall,
Puddles started to freeze until the roads
Became like skating rinks;
Sheets of silver ice shone in the lamplight
Of a dozen streets.

At the start of a new day a thaw has come,
And everywhere the eye can see
The world is wet.

9

The Sun

Morning has come. The sun appears
And as we watch it seems to grow
And slowly lifts into the sky,
A big, round ball that climbs up high
And shines to start a brand-new day.

It seems to leap and dance about
From cloud to cloud, with flickering rays;
It warms the earth and makes us smile,
And keeps us bright and happy while
It dances on its way.

All day it moves across the sky,
Playing a game among the clouds.
First peeping here, then hiding there,
Until we start to wonder where
Its shining face will next appear.

Evening has come and night draws near;
The sun has stopped its merry game.
It's almost time to go to bed,
As yellow changes into red,
And now the sun sinks slowly down.

10

Raindrops

Pitter-patter — patter-pit.
The rain is falling, ever falling.
Hear it drumming on the roof-tops,
Dripping loudly from the gutters.
Plop ... *plop* ... ploppety *plop*.
I wonder, will it ever stop?

All along the streets are puddles.
Big ones, small ones, some like oceans.
Umbrellas shelter dreary faces;
Faces full of discontentment.
Only children still are happy,
Wading in the streaming gutters.

Yet how beautiful a raindrop
As it cascades from the sky.
Perfect, rounded, travelling downward
'Til with miniature explosion
Joins with myriad other raindrops
All to reach their journeys' end.

Listen to the pitter-patter,
Hear the rhythm of the rain.
Hear it drumming on the rooftops,
Dripping loudly from the gutters,
See the children's smiling faces
Catching raindrops as they play.

11

Beginnings

When first we drop a seed into the ground
It disappears from sight and dormant stays
Until the Spring.
Round and small it lies,
Quietly waiting for the warmer days.
Beneath the earth, hid fast from human eyes,
The roots appear,
Thin tendrils spreading outwards.
Then a tiny tip appears above the soil,
Piercing the air and daily rising taller.
The shoots begin to open and to spread
Until we see, enclosed within the bowl,
A bud.
A bud that, opening slowly in the sun,
Reveals a pure, exquisite flower.
What will it be, this flower? A tall and stately iris?
A cup-shaped tulip? A sweetly-scented rose?
Each one a perfectly created form
From such a small and dark
Beginning.

12

A Harvest Prayer

When autumn colours show again
Once more our thoughts begin to turn
To harvest time, and all it means—
Fresh food to eat, warm fires to burn.

We thank you, God, for fishermen
Who brave the perils of the deep,
Casting their nets on storm tossed seas,
Whilst we at home in comfort keep.

We think of men upon the rigs
Who drill for oil so rich and black;
And divers laying miles of pipe
To send their precious harvest back.

And thank you, God, for mining folk
Who toil deep inside the earth,
Swinging their picks in the blackened depths
To bring us coal for life and warmth.

While in our factories people work,
Reaping—for the common good—
The harvest of our great machines,
That make our clothes and give us food.

God, let us not forget these things
When harvest time has come and gone;
But give our thanks, throughout the year,
For those who bring the harvest home.

13

The Elephant and the Ant

Just picture the elephant and the ant
If you saw them side by side.
Such a funny sight it would be,
One small, one big and wide.

The ant is a busy little thing,
Rushing here and there.
He hurries and scurries all the while,
Skittering everywhere.

The elephant, now, is very large
And walks with measured pace,
With long slow steps and swinging trunk
He moves from place to place.

I wonder, should they have a race,
Which one of them would win?
To try and work the problem out
Would have you in a spin!

But *one* thing I am sure about,
And that, my friend is this:
An ant you can hardly see at all,
An elephant you can't miss.

14

Kangaroo Hop

Jumpety-jump, bumpety-bump,
Just see how the kangaroo moves:
He jumps and he bounces all the day long.
As he goes on his way he sings us his song—
  Hippety, hippety hop.

Leapety-leap, leapety-leap,
It must be fun to travel that way,
Leaping and hopping and jumping along,
Bounding about all the day.
  Hippety, hippety hop.

Jumpety-jump, bumpety-bump,
See just how high he can leap:
Hopping along just as fast as he can
You'd never catch him however you ran.
  Hippety, hippety hop.

Leapety-leap, leapety-leap,
I wish I could go for a ride
On the kangaroo's back for an hour or two
And travel the land far and wide.
  Hippety, hippety hop.

15

The Kestrel

Look! There in the sky up high, very high,
A bird in the light of the sun.
See how he hovers and flutters his wings
And gazes intently down at the ground,
While seeming to hang in the sky.

Look! There in the field, way down below,
A mouse on a tussock of grass.
See how he twitters and wrinkles his whiskers
And gazes intently down at the ground
(While doing his toilet — you know!).

A mouse and a bird — a bird and a mouse.
Each one looking for dinner.
Look out little mouse for danger is lurking,
Run, for your life is at stake!
Run to your safe little house.

With a whoosh and a swoosh the kestrel swoops down.
He rushes from out of the sky
And lands on the tussock of grass with a pounce
And stabs at the mouse with his sharp, rounded beak.
But all he gets is a mouthful of grass......
For the mouse is now back in 'Mouse Town'.

16

Snake Song

Slither and slide, wriggle and glide,
That's how I move, says the snake.
I stay on my stomach and travel along
And as I travel I sing me a song
That's certain to keep you awake.

Rattle and roll, rattle and roll,
You can hear me from miles away.
They say that my rattle can frighten a man
And make him run as fast as he can
If only to keep me at bay.

Twist and twirl, screw and curl,
I can wind myself into a ball.
I can make myself small, although I am strong,
And yet I can stretch until I am long,
Or even rise to be tall.

Hiss and spit, hiss and spit,
My tongue is as long as my head.
And if I pounce and shoot out that tongue
It's certain that you wouldn't last very long,
But I think I'll just sleep instead!

17

At Snail's Pace

Slowly the snail inches forward,
Carrying his house upon his back.
Behind he leaves a silvery trail
That winds and twists with each new turn he makes.

He moves so smoothly over soil or stone
That almost nothing seems to happen.
Yet the silvery track grows longer
As he passes on his way.

How hard to move at snail's pace,
To lift each foot so carefully
That not a sound is heard, nor movement felt in space
As the body smoothly stretches out
To follow the path the snail takes.

Then when journeying is done to
Draw inside oneself and smaller, smaller curl
Like the snail withdrawing into his shell
And shutting out the world.

18

Journey into Space

5, 4, 3, 2, 1 — Zero!

Slowly, like some monstrous bird, the space ship lifts into the sky,
Rising with strength and purpose higher, yet still higher,
Until it moves beyond the range of human eyes
And into regions yet unknown
That wait still to be conquered by the minds of men.

Onward it goes, past stars and planets, other realms,
Regions of mystery where who knows what may exist.
Maybe a life as civilized as ours,
Or the haunts of robots, green-eyed monsters,
Creatures from another world.

Inside the capsule space men work,
Moving from place to place with springy step,
Lifting, floating, drifting in strange air,
Looking themselves like some peculiar beings come from space,
Working towards their journey's end.

Then touchdown and an open door into another world,
A barren place strewn wide with rocks,
A mass of shapes and sizes,
Sharp and jagged or smooth and round as if worn out by time.
No sound is heard or movement seen,
Only the lift and fall of the space man's step.

Then, mission fulfilled, exploring done,
The capsule slowly climbs up into space
Towards a marriage with the mother ship
And safe return
To float down from eternity to earth
And splashdown.

19

A Seaside Day

Slowly the sun lifts over the rim of the sea,
Lightening the darkness of the water,
Until the rippling waves reflect the sky's pure blue
And a new and perfect day has dawned.

The light shines through the water, wakening the fish
And sends them darting here and there
Like small, bright lights, between sharp, jagged rocks
Seeming like teeth grown on the ocean bed.

Above the water waves roll gently to the shore
And then creep slowly back as if
An unseen magnet pulls them, joins them with the sea,
And sends them rushing to the sand once more.

On days like this the beach echoes the sound of children's voices
Playing the seaside games all children love,
Whilst on the water a myriad boats with sails spread
Wait to catch the first rising of the wind.

Towards the middle of the afternoon the sun goes in
And big, black clouds move slowly closer from the west;
The wind, now like a roaring lion, sends the waves
Crashing loudly down upon the shore.

Time to haul in the boats! So lend a hand;
Pull 'til each one is safely on the beach,
Away from the savage pounding of the water,
Safe 'til the start of another seaside day.

Quick as it came, the storm begins to pass,
And as the daylight fades the sea becomes once more
A place of shadows, until as darkness falls
Only the gentle lapping of the waves disturbs the silence.

20

Bonfire Night

Listen to the fire and feel its warmth.
Magical flickering flames lighting the sky.
The night is alive with a hundred sights and sounds.
The noise of the crackling fire
And curling flames creeping towards the guy
Destined to burn.
The whoosh and swoop of a rocket as it shoots into the sky,
Bursting into a cluster of lights,
Bright against the darkness.
The whizz and swirl of the catherine wheel
Turning upon its pole,
Spinning and whirling, spiralling—twirling
Round and round with a spit and a spat.
Beautiful cascades of roman candle, silver fountain, golden rain,
Colour, light and the gentle flow of falling stars.
Sharp cracking sound of the rip-rap,
Zig-zagging its way across the ground,
Spiky and sudden—this way and that.
And over all the sound of childrens' voices
Calling, laughing, cheering—
Part of the wonderful sights and sounds of bonfire night.

21

Late for Work

Tucked up warm and fast asleep,
Wandering in the land of dreams,
While the daylight, filtering through,
Says good-bye to moonlight beams.

Suddenly a harsh, loud ring,
What a noise! It's that alarm.
Pull the bedclothes overhead —
A minute more will do no harm.

Stretch and turn and slowly lift
One leg, two legs out of bed.
It's time to rise and face the day;
Stir yourself, you sleepy-head.

Goodness me! Is that the time?
You'll have to rush to catch the train.
Wash yourself and get dressed quick
Or you'll be late for work again.

There's no time for breakfast now —
Through the door and close the gate;
To the station just in time
To hear them say, 'Your train is late!'

Sit a moment, catch your breath;
Watch the signals rise and drop.
Metal pointers, sharp and sudden,
Tell you that your train will stop.

Now, at last, the train is coming.
Hear the whistle! Clear the way!
Look at all the people rushing —
You won't find a seat to-day.

As the engine gathers speed,
Fields and hedgerows all rush by.
Horses grazing, rather frightened,
Gallop off, manes tossing high.

Why not walk down to the buffet—
Have a morning cup of tea?
Rattling train makes footsteps falter,
Rolls you like the waves at sea.

Here's your station! There's no time now—
Morning tea will have to wait.
You must make a resolution—
'To-morrow you will *not* be late!'

22

The Fairground

The sun is shining overhead
And birds are singing in the trees.
'Come on, children! Out of bed
And hurry down to breakfast, please.'

It couldn't be a better day
For our visit to the fair.
The sooner we get on our way
The quicker we will all be there.

Off we go now to the 'bus.
'Jump on there—seats free on top!'
Won't the people envy us,
Eating sweets and drinking pop.

How long the journey seems to take,
But now at last we're nearly there.
Through the turnstile, past the lake,
And we can only stand and stare.

For there ahead—oh, what a sight!
The busy fairground is alive
With bustle, laughter, sound and light—
Another world of make-believe.

First the helter-skelter drop.
Collect your mat and up you go,
Climb the steps right to the top.
Then whizzing round and round you go,

Spiralling back to the ground
To reach the bottom with a bump.
You find you are so quickly down,
A sudden stop that makes you jump.

Climb up on the roundabout,
Feel the horses rise and fall.
Some are thin and some are stout
And some don't look like a horse at all.

Let's go to the hall of mirrors
And laugh at all the shapes we make.
Sue's as fat as two wide doors,
While Johnny looks like a garden rake.

Where are all those people going?
Look! A strong man doing tricks.
See his muscles, firm and flowing,
Lifting that great pile of bricks.

We'd like to stay and watch some more,
But there's so much for us to see.
Look! The clock says almost 'one'.
How hungry we all seem to be.

Dinner done, what shall we do?
'Something quiet,' Mother says.
We're feeling rather lazy, too,
And so we'll simply sit and gaze

At all the fascinating sights,
The swing boats and the ferris wheel,
The ghost train with its flashing lights,
And wonder how the people feel

Who dare to venture through its doors.
One last go! What shall it be?
Hurry now and choose, because
It's time to go back home for tea.

Clamber onto the big dipper,
Feel it whooshing up and down,
Climbing slowly, ever higher,
Then rushing down towards the ground.

It's time that we were on our way.
Just think of all the sights we've seen.
What a way to end the day,
And such a lovely day it's been!

23

Giantland

There is a place I've heard about.
A land that's far away.
I'd love to go and visit there
If only for a day,

To see the trees that reach so high
And flowers that grow as tall as men
They almost seem to touch the sky
And then look twice as tall again.

Now you should see the people there
They are so very strong.
The strangest people anywhere,
As wide as they are long.

Their legs are like the trunks of trees,
Their bodies like balloons.
They say that when they take their ease
They fill up several rooms.

You'd wonder at each meal they eat,
A most tremendous feast.
They must be hollow to their feet,
Or to their knees at least!

They walk with very heavy tread,
Most ponderous and slow,
And spend a lot of time in bed
(To build their strength, you know.)

I'm sure you know the place I mean.
It has a special name,
And marvellous wonders to be seen
Of great and special fame.

For everything is huge and vast
And also very grand.
It has to be this way you see,
For this is Giantland.

24

Tiny-Wee

He's such a tiny little man
Who never ever grows.
There's hardly even been a space
Between his tootsies and his nose.

Because he's small, he's very light
And never makes a sound.
He sings and dances on his way
With feet that hardly touch the ground.

At night when he is very tired,
He curls himself for sleep
Into a weeny little ball,
And so still does he keep.

You wouldn't know that he is there,
So very small is he,
That all the people hereabouts
Have named him Tiny-Wee.

Now Tiny is a happy man,
Just seven inches high,
Who likes to dance along all day
To see if he can reach the sky.

He'll skip and hop and jump and trot,
He'll gallop and he'll run.
He hardly every walks at all
'Cos that just isn't any fun.

But even though he tries so hard
To stretch up to the sky,
He doesn't grow another inch
And here's the reason why.

It isn't very strange you know.
Not really strange at all.
For 'Tiny' is a little elf,
And after all, *all* elves are small.

25

Dancing Shoes

When you put on dancing shoes
Your feet will come alive
And you can move in lots of ways
Although you're only five.

You can run with tiny steps,
Making patterns in and out,
Movement forwards, backwards, sideways
And sometimes turning right about.

You can gallop like a horse,
Or maybe you would like to trot,
Then you can hop from foot to foot
About the room or on the spot.

Skip and lift your knees up high
Or walk with giant stride.
Jump with little bouncy jumps
And now with feet stretched wide.

You can do so many things
Although you're only five
'Cos when you put on dancing shoes
Your feet will come alive.

26

A Witchy Tale

It's the night of the witches' party;
The woods are cold and black.
The wind is blowing through the trees
And leaves are whispering in the breeze
As we creep along the track.

As the clock on the village church tower chimes
The witches begin to wake.
With spiky fingers and crooked nose
And jiggedy-jaggedy heels and toes
They dance until daybreak.

Just look at their cloaks and pointed hats,
And hear them laugh and shout,
As they dance around the crackling fire
And make the flames leap higher and higher
And cast their spells about.

It's the night of the witches' party
And every witch is here.
But where they come from nobody knows
For as soon as a glimmer of daylight shows
Every one will disappear.

27

Strange Creature

Oily sea monster.
Long slimy tendrils twisting, coiling, reaching out,
Intertwining, one with another.
Gliding through water
Black with the inky darkness of the sunless depths.
The tendrils close with sudden spasms
The scent of danger, close—unseen
Contracts the body,
And it hangs, momentarily suspended,
Then opening out resumes its journey through the unknown wastes.
Giant octopus, huge, ungainly,
Moving soundlessly through the water
An unknown, nameless monster of the deep.

28

Jerky the Puppet

Jerky's a little man made out of wood.
He moves in a very strange way,
And if you don't help him to pick himself up
He'll stay fast asleep all the day.

He has lots of strings on his hands and his feet
And some joined to other parts, too.
If you pull very hard on the strings one by one
You'll see just what Jerky can do.

He can grow bit by bit 'til he's standing up high
And make himself seem very tall,
But if you let go of the strings one by one
He can curl up again, very small.

When Jerky moves it's a wonderful sight,
For all of him dances, you know;
His head and his middle, his elbows and knees,
And even his big, wooden toe.

Yes, Jerky's a little made made out of wood.
He moves in a very strange way,
And if you don't help him to pick himself up
He'll stay fast asleep all the day.

29

The Swing

Higher, higher—swing me high.
Swing me upwards through the air.
And should you swing me high enough
Perhaps I might reach to the sky,
And look with wonder all around.
Then swing me low—oh, swing me low—
Until I come back down to earth
And feel my feet upon the ground.

O what joy it is to go
Backwards and forwards, up and down,
Like a giant swooping bird,
First soaring high, then rushing low.
My swing is like an aeroplane.
It takes me flying through the sky,
And having carried me so high
It brings me safely down again.

30

My Flying Kite

Gently and with infinite care
The string unravels from his grasp.
The kite lifts smoothly up into the sky,
A fragile thing
Which seems to hang suspended for a moment
Then begins to rise,
Slowly increasing the ever-widening gap
'Twixt earth and sky.

The kite is free, riding upon the currents of the air,
Lifting and falling with the changing wind.
The boy is moving, too,
Guiding the kite upon the string,
Feeling the pull of the wind
Under his hand.
For me, watching, nothing exists but the boy,
The kite, and a feeling of freedom
As my heart rises and soars
With the wind.
Now, with a sudden change, the wind drops
And for a moment all is still,
But in the lull,
Like a giant bird intent upon its prey,
The kite comes swooping down
Out of the sky
Its magic gone,
And I must wait for another day
To feel the lifting of my heart
And the freedom of the wind.

31

Catrina

Catrina is my dancing doll.
She wears a dress of pink,
And a small pair of ballet shoes
To help her dance upon her toes.

Her steps are light and dainty
As she spins and pirouettes,
And dances now both high and low,
First whirling fast, now curving slow.

Some times she leaps into the air
With legs and arms outstretched,
And lifted chest and head held high
So pleasing to my watching eye.

And often in my sleep I dream
That I might dance like her
As lightly and as dainty too.
Perhaps one day I'll dance for you.

O how I'd like to dance like her
And wear a dress of pink,
And leap and turn so gracefully,
Just like Catrina does for me.

Perhaps one day not far ahead
If I should practice hard
And do all that I'm taught to do
Then maybe I will dance for you.

32

Bouncing Balls

Bounce, bounce; thump, thump—
Pat—pat—pat—pat ...

Have you listened to the sound
A bouncing ball makes on the ground?
You bounce it high, you bounce it low,
You bounce it quick or bounce it slow.

Big balls make a thumping noise,
Just right for football-loving boys.
Rubber balls go pit-a-pat.
Little girls love them just like that.

Bounce it up against the wall.
You can watch it rise and fall,
And hear it make a different sound
As it drops back to the ground.

Bounce with right and left hand too,
You can bounce not one but two,
Bounce them forwards, to the side,
Near to you, then very wide.

Bounce them high and bounce them low,
Sometimes quick and sometimes slow,
Have you listened to the sound
A bouncing ball makes on the ground?

Bounce, bounce; thump, thump —
Pat — pat — pat — pat.

33

Balloon

O what a strange and shrivelled thing
Is lying in my hand.
Whatever can it be, you say —
It's hard to understand.
But if I put it to my lips
And gently start to blow,
Then what a change we now behold,
For it begins to grow.

Little by little, inch by inch,
It stretches firm and tight,
Until it makes a big, round ball—
A most amazing sight.
But if I blow a bit too much
I'll burst my big balloon,
And the happiness it gives me
Will melt away too soon.

So when it's just a perfect size
I'll tie it up with string
And fasten to the washing line
A gaily-coloured thing
That drifts and sways from side to side
And dances in the breeze
While reaching outwards on the string
To cast small shadows on the trees.

Then when I've watched it for a while
I'll slip the knot I tied
And let it drift away from me
To travel far and wide,
'Til lifting ever higher now
It passes from my sight
And my balloon has flown away,
Balloon so round and bright.

And now I wish I'd left it there
To dance upon it's string,
And yet I know that it appeared
A sad and lonely thing.
I had to let it go, you see,
To watch it soaring high,
For now its found a grand new home—
'Balloon land' in the sky!

34

My Magic Box

In my bedroom I have a box
Painted a beautiful shiny red.
It lives in a cupboard big and tall,
Just beside my cosy bed.

Sometimes I open my shiny box
And give myself a big surprise;
And if you could see what is there inside
You really wouldn't believe your eyes:

For it's a magic Jack in the box.
When I open the lid it shoots up high.
It is so very big and strong
I think it's going to reach the sky.

Sometimes it jumps right out of the box
And bounces and zig-zags all over the floor,
And I think if I didn't catch it quick
It would jump right away from me out of the door.

Then, when it's tired from bouncing along,
I pick it up and I put it away.
Then I close the lid of my shiny box
And leave it to rest 'til another day.

35

The Rocking Horse

I had a little rocking horse
Made of wood and painted grey.
Sometimes I climbed upon its back
And made it rock and felt it sway.

But when it was time to go to bed
And I was fast asleep at night,
My rocking horse, it came alive
And pranced and frisked 'til the morning light.

It jumped off its rockers and galloped away
With legs aquiver and tossing head.
It loved to be free and enjoy itself
When it knew I was fast asleep in bed.

Yet when the daylight came peeping through
Then back to its rockers it quickly came,
And quietly waited for night to fall
'Till rocking horse time came round again!

36

The Mirror Game

Look at me looking at you.
Whatever I do you must do it too.
My reflection you must be, and
You must always copy me.

I nod my head, you nod yours too.
It doesn't matter what I do.
Hold your hands up, lift them high,
Together we'll reach towards the sky.

Hunch your shoulders up and down.
Do a spin and turn around.
Stretch your arms out big and wide,
Drop them quickly to your side.

Can you make a shape like this,
Arms and legs all in a twist,
Stretch up to be straight and tall
Or curl yourself up very small?

Now, perhaps, I'll choose to grow
Moving really smooth and slow.
Or I'll bounce up like a ball
Then, like a rag doll, down I'll fall.

Do you like to play this game
Where we always do the same?
You must watch me carefully,
If you want to move like me.

37

Machines

Switching on, starting up.
Hear the voice of the machine.
Engines busy, moving faster,
Gaining power every minute.
Listen to that busy sound.

Clickety-click tickety-tick
Says the voice of the machine.
Rods and pistons, sharp and sudden,
Moving always, never stopping,
Forwards, backwards, up and down.

Whizz and whirl, twist and twirl,
Says the voice of the machine.
Wheels and more wheels, smooth and flowing,
Moving always, never stopping,
Spinning, turning, round and round.

Reaching out, switching off.
Hear the voice of the machine.
Engines stopping, growing quiet,
Getting slower every minute,
Winding, gently winding down.

38

Walking

Tiny steps up on your toes,
Touch the ceiling with your nose.
That's the way you want to be—
  Come walk by me.

Bend your knees and walk down low,
Feet together, keep it slow.
That's the way you want to be—
  So walk with me.

Stretch and do a giant stride,
Make your steps reach big and wide.
That's the way you want to be—
  Please walk by me.

Step and match the steady beat,
Walk on heels and sides of feet.
That's the way you want to be—
  Come stay with me.

39

The Tight-Rope Walker

A sharp intake of breath
Ripples across the circus ring
As, high above, the tight-rope walker plays his game with death.
Beyond him only the shadow of the canvas roof,
Beneath, row upon row of faces peering up,
Eyes bright with excitement,
Yet so very still.
Slowly he moves across his rope.
With arms outstretched, his balance keeps,
Each step so perfect; forward, back, around.
First low then high; with careful measured tread
So lightly feels his way from end to end,
That for a moment, it would seem, he hangs suspended
Out of space.
His body bends and then with sudden jerk
He turns a perfect somersault,
To settle safely on the rope once more.
Now trick upon trick he does,
Each one more daring than the one before.
Hands grip, eyes stare — the audience waits
To see if he can possibly survive upon that narrow rope,
Made like a gossamer thread.
At last the act comes to an end,
And through the silence in the circus ring
We hear the sound of indrawn breath released
And the sudden clapping of each pair of hands.

Index of First Lines